more praise for

SON OF BYFORD

"The word 'outspoken' is so weak when applied to Juba Kalamka—
'real-spoken' is much closer. His personal/cultural narrative work in
Son of Byford sinks in deep by being just that—so goddamn real. The
spoken part is there too—this is hybrid verbal work...these words fly off
the page into your face and ears with all kinds of language, preaching
and sextalking, marking history and erasures, summoning, enacting
and embodying a frank lingua, sounding blood and truth."

Richard Loranger
author of *Unit of Agency*

"Punk and delicious / Faggot and viscous / A boy who is cunt / No
longer fictitious."

Dazié Grego-Sykes
author of *Black Faggotry*

NOMADIC PRESS

OAKLAND

PHILADELPHIA

XALAPA

WWW.NOMADICPRESS.ORG

MASTHEAD

FOUNDING PUBLISHER
J. K. Fowler

ASSOCIATE EDITOR
Michaela Mullin

LEAD EDITOR
Noelia Cerna

DESIGN
Jevohn Tyler Newsome

MISSON STATEMENT Through publications, events, and active community participation, Nomadic Press collectively weaves together platforms for intentionally marginalized voices to take their rightful place within the world of the written and spoken word. Through our limited means, we are simply attempting to help right the centuries' old violence and silencing that should never have occurred in the first place and build alliances and community partnerships with others who share a collective vision for a future far better than today.

INVITATIONS Nomadic Press wholeheartedly accepts invitations to read your work during our open reading period every year. To learn more or to extend an invitation, please visit: www.nomadicpress.org/invitations

DISTRIBUTION
Orders by teachers, libraries, trade bookstores, or wholesalers:

Nomadic Press Distribution
orders@nomadicpress.org
(510) 500-5162

Small Press Distribution
spd@spdbooks.org
(510) 524-1668 / (800) 869-7553

This book was made possible by a loving community of chosen family and friends, old and new.

For author questions or to book a reading at your bookstore, university/school, or alternative establishment, please send an email to info@nomadicpress.org.

Cover art: "Blue Figure" by Wardell McNeal

Published by Nomadic Press, 111 Fairmount Avenue, Oakland, California 94611

First printing, 2022

Library of Congress Cataloging-in-Publication Data

Title: *Son of Byford*
p. cm.

Summary: *Son of Byford* is a meandering mining of meaning from the memory of many middle passages. This collection refracts 1970s shades of Black and blues that give way to hip hop, post-millennium tensions, and godless queer queryings, informed by love, conviction, and hope.

[1. POETRY / American / African American & Black. 2. POETRY / LGBTQ+. 3. POETRY / Subjects & Themes / Love & Erotica. 4. POETRY / Subjects & Themes / Death, Grief, Loss. 5. POETRY / American / General.] I. III. Title.

LIBRARY OF CONGRESS CONTROL NUMBER: 2022937159

ISBN: 978-1-955239-31-8

SON OF BYFORD

SON OF BYFORD

**NOMADIC
PRESS**

Oakland · Philadelphia · Xalapa

for Twila Mae Hillard Rambus
aka "Aunt Dit"
(1931–1992)
in unions there is strength

contents

notes

reading guide

foreword

Sometime in the mid-2000s, I submitted a copy of my sophomore album, *The Muse,* to *Colorlines* magazine for review. It was around the same time that I first heard the pioneering work of Deep Dickollective (D/DC), co-founded by Juba Kalamka. Finding D/DC at that particular moment was crucial for me as a gay boy born into a white evangelical family who spent my teens and twenties immersed in the Black Pentecostal tradition.

D/DC's philosophical brilliance, audacity, and connection to the world I came from gave me the courage to speak my truth in both my life and my art while not completely chopping off my roots. As synchronicity tends to work, *Colorlines* did, indeed, review my album and the review was written by Juba! If memory serves correctly, we connected on MySpace shortly thereafter and have remained friends, collaborators, and comrades for over fifteen years since.

Son of Byford encapsulates and expands on what Juba's work—in D/DC, as a solo recording artist, performance artist, poet, and, most recently, in his band COMMANDO—has always been about in a large sense: curiosity and complication. Utilizing his deep knowledge of the most well-known and lesser-known contributors to Black culture, he wants you to remember Jack Baker, Johnnie Keyes, Mattie Moss Clark, Black films of the 1970s (celebrated so especially beautifully in "Re/membering Mamuwalde"), and grapple with how Sid Ordower's Chicago-based gospel music television program *Jubilee Showcase* connects with the exploration of living outside of binary framing (right/wrong, gay/straight, Christian/other, God/Devil). What does one have to do with the other? Well, that's what Juba wants you to think about.

Throughout the poems contained in this collection, Kalamka's traverse through faith communities and their histories is essential to note. Yes, he can talk church folk and gospel music, but he can also speak the language of the Nation of Islam and its history. He knows of the orishas. They are placed alongside each other and discussed simultaneously, in dialogue with one another. He juxtaposes this insider knowledge with his otherness. To less-complex thinkers, his identities should conflict with the ways those communities are a part of him, but he contemplates that experience and his truth as a means of disturbing the peace, insisting *Yes. This AND This belong in the same conversation.* He blurs the lines between the (perceived) blasphemous and the audacious, forcing us to consider why we've made so many cows sacred and why we've called things filthy that are quite holy.

There's also a kind of space/time memory that *Son of Byford* invokes. For those of us old enough to have been in similar spaces, the poems awaken a palpable remembering of feeling/knowing before there were words and representation to mirror our stories back to us. When we felt alone. When we weren't normal. When we believed we might have been the only people in the world attracted in the ways that we were. The days before the internet. When porn was not just a click away. When bathroom cruising was an art. When those experiences were not recorded on a cell phone but had to be retained in one's memory for recall later. When time moved slower and our conundrums did not need to be so quickly resolved, identified, and saleable. In Reinaldo

Arenas' *Before Night Falls*, Arenas acknowledged the rights attained by "homosexual militancy," but he also mourned the new kinds of division that emerged as a result of these gains. In the pages of this collection, this tension is present and explored. For younger readers, these memories are an invitation to feel and see differently, away from too-bright screens, push notifications, and the inundation of social media content.

In the tradition of Ntozake Shange and Essex Hemphill, Juba Kalamka utilizes poetry as bibliography, historical narrative, and autobiography as a means to point us to the past to more deeply contemplate the present. Read and re-read the poems. Travel with them. Circle the names, places, books, and films to research later and let this work infiltrate and expand *your* world. Most importantly, allow yourself to connect with the anxieties, angers, joys, losses, complexities, desires, bodies, and orgasms that *Son of Byford* invites you to discover.

Tim Dillinger
author of *God's Music Is My Life* on Substack,
Editorial Content Manager for soulmusic.com

May 9, 2022
Nashville, Tennessee

introduction

As a child of the Great African-American Migration and Diaspora, my life has been contextualized by a myriad of city/country/city stories steeped in narratives of struggle and overcoming. My mixed class-up-bringing (Mom from sharecroppers-cum-storefront rummage sale owners and single mom night continuation high school grad and self taught artist and performer; Dad of West Virginia coal mining colored camp denizens, escaping through military service to college and a career as a school teacher) was the material for 1970s post-MLK-rebellion-Africentrist-education stories of greatness and hero histories, but also the space where narratives that didn't neatly or comfortably fit (paternal Grandma's struggling with mental health, dying in a fire with an eight-year-old cousin you know from a single photo, the maternal Grandpaw with the second family who you don't meet 'til your 12th birthday, the gay cousin who left the fold decades ago and is somewhere in one of the towns where you today teach medical students).

I named this collection *Son of Byford* in part because of the happenstance of it being the title of a favorite song by Run-DMC released in the middle of my high school years and the name of the first public elementary school I attended (William H. Byford Elementary on Chicago's far west side).

A poet friend remarked upon seeing class photos of me at the Africentrist school I attended from 1974–77 (homemade dashiki and cut-offs, unsmiling, arms folded in child soldier-readiness) and a class photo taken at Byford (favorite green cords, favorite ugly blue Christmas sweater, wide and glowing smile) in April and October 1977, respectively:

"Wow! Looks like integration did you some good!" they wrote. I had never looked at the photos in quite that way before. They were certainly separate social, cultural, and emotional planets for me. Both were significant, but neither had merited deeper examination, partly because the geographic distance between where each photo was taken was so short.

That joking observation, that unintentional prompting of self-reflection was an amazing gift, as it became the engine and guiding intent of this collection—an intentional look at my movement inside of movements inside of Movements; how they informed and continue to inform my self-concept, and my front-of-mind notions of where I want to move next—as an artist, as a person, as a member of overlapping and intersecting communities and communions. And how my underlying compulsion (Duty? Obligation? Mission?) to serve for the better, for better or worse, is evolving.

Dr. William Heath Byford (1817-1890) was co-founder of the American Gynecological Society and the Chicago Medical College, chair of the Department of Obstetrics and Diseases of Women at Rush Medical College, and was considered the foremost gynecologist of his day and a champion of medical education for women.

I very much understand the lack of importance for teachers, staff, and community members to inquire as to his identity accomplishments, and larger racialized and gendered consequence any more than one would for another (presumably) random Old White Man namesake of a neighborhood school. Yet and still the context, complications and connections are not lost on me.

I learned of Byford's medical career about two years prior to writing this. Not long before that I was given a frame for my familial narratives around my great-great-great-great maternal grandfather Washington Towns' ownership of my great-great-great grandmother Anna Mae Towns, and it became even more important for me to contribute a more than facile rendering of yet another intensely complicated narrative of African American experience.

The collapse of patriarchal naming of the womb/portal/time machine that was Byford Elementary (demolished in 1999, the year I left Chicago for the San Francisco Bay Area, and replaced with the Milton Brunson Specialty School-named for the late longtime pastor of the church across the street) is of a density that cannot be parsed in this introduction.

I hope the survival, service, and storytelling I've attempted to engage with in this collection can serve as the basis for connection to some of the past realities and lives that were enabled the interventions of others who similarly saw their way to the just- be that through the parallel arts of community health advocacy and education I've had the opportunity to contribute to, or the gentle rubbing back to life my maternal great grandmother Oray Booker Washington performing on my infantile paralyzed three-year-old mother in 1943 that insured I would have the opportunity to work out my own wrinkles, in time. Thank you for making it this far with me, and I hope these pages can be a part of the engine that gets you closer to where you want to go.

Juba Kalamka

An Ode To No-Hearts (Pulse)

every time you were silent
[laughed? Actively co-signed?]
when your friends and coworkers told
trans bathroom jokes
faggot jokes bulldagga jokes
jokes about black and brown queers
about damnation
about the deservedness

about how your God don't like ugly
approves of murder and massacre
of Maricon and Mariposa
[that day I was riding the #1 the security guard church lady said
"I blame her" when they left Gwen Araujo in a ditch]

every joke
every professional opinion
about bisexual vectors of disease
that you choked on
because i didn't Look Like A Faggot
when you meant
i look like i could
and would
beat you to death with my fists

like you're safe because
the cisheteronormative
violins of sex
won't play their tune on your head

every time you gave amens
clapped up preacher pigfoot
in a hood tabernacle
or white mega church

or polite progressive meetings
led by understanding straight men
or Dashikified December Harambes
at the local junior college
because geles woven

of the fabric of internalized racism
are thought to be bulletproof
because when the nigga truck comes
the storm trooper with the clipboard
will skip past the straight-acting

my fivehead is big
but cannot hold this moment's Maafa
and I'm tired of my anger
evaporating my tears

and i might rewrite
because I'm feeling incoherent
and don't know what to do when
I get out of bed

but I don't think I'll get shot
before i go brush my teeth
so I will get up and get out
find out where the colored children
are gathering
pour some

and try not
to glare too much in the train
tomorrow
or at the TSA on Tuesday
despite wanting to breathe
and keep my eyeballs
from getting choked out of their sockets

because I'm getting less and less capable
of holding it down
holding on
hanging on the ledge
while The Good People
the very well meaning ones
step on my finger

An Eminem's Front

Mrs. Liuzzo (Vi)
Ain't Die
For Tim Wise
Or Rachel's Lie

Dark Brother

(for John Anthony Bailey aka Jack Baker, 1947–1994)

Jack Baker
pulled up next to me in his Wonderbug
Red fender fisheye reflection
Making my seven year old blow pop head Look even bigger
He say
I saw you watching me
Las' Saturday mornin', man
You got that whop-sided mini- fro
Jus' like mine. You wanna ride?
It'll blow your mind awayyyyyy.

I do my secret agent jump-in with both feet
Then push the magic horn
It smells like the half chewed bubblegum
that he used to stick it to the dash
How's it feel to be me, dude, he said
Pressing for a laugh
With his trademark Tommish yowsa grin
Ummm... I don't know yet, I blurted
How many monies they pay you on the Supershow?
This many, he say, holding up two fingers
Then fished a dollar out of his pocket and gave it to me

You gotta pay to play bruh-thuh, he say
So cool supercool running a palm backward Across his nappy head
Now you halfway there

Jack Baker's momma cooked us some
Fingerlickinggoodness
She say *that ain't his real name*
Jus' one that sounds more like an actor
Call him Mister Hollywood, she say
Spooning a crusty corner
Of macaroni on my plate
My sister call that part "the booty"
There's four of them
In a skillet of cornbread
If you cut it right
Momma wrap caramel sheet cake
In napkins and dixies
And stick it in her purse at church
He watch and learn that Jack
He can make you smile with the taste good
Even when he's all of a hot mess
On the inside

Jack Baker, according to Garry Marshall
Was the only black man living in Milwaukee in 1956
Never mind Aaron, Bruton, Mantilla,
Or Pizzaro

There really were a few Brave ones,
Quiet as it is kept
A group of fresh faced kids
From a good family
Found him on the steps
In front of the high school
And decided to let him play djembe
In their band
He told them his name was "Sticks"
Because he thought that was a good name
For a negro drummer to have
Hanging out with the fellas was a big deal
Back when Italians, Jews, Greeks
And the Irish weren't white people yet
Still jammed between the rock and hard
Of truth and consequence
And the nostalgia that is by definition
A lack of memory

I like eating the Pancho's Special at Mel's
Jack like the pancakes
And though when I remember
As we dine in the in the midst
Of a cacophony of doo-wop fetishism
That he and I
Wouldn't have been allowed to eat here
During their Happy Days

[No, not even in San Francisco.]
I can't go back to the future just yet
I have to linger
I need to remind the waitress
Who clearly doesn't want to serve us
This tattoo freak hiding the stars and arrows
Under a long sleeved flair-riddled blouse
Manic Panicked 'do all pulled in a bun
That we will not go away
And that when they come,
They will come for her too
And they will laugh at the idea
That she thought they would not see her

Jack gave it the old college try
I think his failure was less a
Right place/wrong time thing
And more the reality
That the ofays had their scrilla solvent
By mid-decade
And now wanted their movies back.
Among hairy asses and seventies bush
Real acting ability
Stands out like a hard cock
So does the moxie it takes
To make it fun when it's clear
They are funning you.

Thirteen and about to bust
Every minute of the day it seems
I keep Jergens and Noxema in business
Because I haven't learned to stroke it slow
Or with a dry hand
Though that skill will come with time

Jack Baker was fly
In his knockoff Members Only
Truckershaded cool belies his
Coke-borne blearyness
Holding court in a dice game
Swilling port wine with my cousin Paul
We real cool/we real/cool
Cool
Jack understands what it means
To taste for white women and
Black dick at the same time
Pats my back
Salves the wounds I got for betraying
Incense and Dashiki-isms
Don't let them out-nigga you, he say
Don't let them out-nigga you
And handed me his Redblackandgreenliberation smoking jacket.
We laughed
And he phone ordered a rib tip dinner
With extra mild

It's all pink inside bruh man.
And the rest don't matter when the lights out
He say through a mouth fulla meat,
Then outta nowhere
Grabs me up by both wrists
And sucks the barbecue sauce
From my thumbs.
They been fucking with you with that Kwanzaa shit, man, he say
You think they be eatin' three-bean salad in Nigeria?
Nigga, that's bull-shit!

When he got all skinny
Most everyone pretended not to notice
He was never a big dude anyways
And the weight loss just made him
More jesterish
But then his skin turned gray
As a Yankees road uniform
And he stopped fucking alla sudden
Ten, twelve movies in a row
With no shit-talking during the blowjob
Noone-liners and double-entendre
During the double-penetration
His head a Dia De La Muerte
Brown sugar skull
Playing only the lascivious old coot

Because the pancake base can't hide it all
Because this shade of purple shows through black
And the goofy overalls
Keep him from looking too outta place
Like he got it   But he did
Have   It   something   else
Enough   to go backwards, some would say
Slumming
As the money people would call it
Jack made it appear as a conscious mapping Of career trajectory
Mathematic calculation of
The cumshot's arc the Betacam
Even after flesh is rent from soul by
Immunoinefficiency
With no last gasp or choke
With him begging the Schlepcar to start
Save a four hour megatape
In the corner of my mind
I close my eyes and watch him
Wonderbugging
Through the San Fernando Valley
Outta-sighteous
Mouth too slick
Tongue too quick
Pimp Hand
Strong

Julyteenth

He had these 25-years-long dreadlocks and couldn't be bothered to go to the salon. He didn't trim his beard. He was a fag. He called himself a fag. He was fat. He was bisexual. He was a sex worker. He wore a dress on a stage at Gay Pride. He mean-mugged me while making my latte at Starbucks in February 2003. He didn't answer me quickly enough when I asked for more coffee stirrers at the cafe station at Starbucks in August 1999. He had a 22-year-old man die in his arms following a drive-by shooting in the hallway of his apartment building while the man's wife and sister watched in September 1995. He received a summons from Cook County when he was behind on his child support in May 1997. He was a rapper. He was a queer rapper. He rapped with other queer rappers who's group name we'll say is unprintable here but has been printed a zillion places. He had sex with a lot of people - too many people. He had sex with people who were HIV-positive. He had sex at sex parties. He had sex in public. He smoked the marijuanas. He ate the marijuana candy. He did some other drugs too. He liked the drugs. He had white girlfriends. He had white boyfriends. He was non monogamous. He was divorced. He moved to the San Francisco Bay Area when his kid was just four years old. He said nigga a lot. He had another kid with a queer woman who he only married after they'd been together for eight years when the kid was six years old and only then because he was going to do his rapper thing in Europe and wanted to have some protection for his "wife" and kid on the cheap. He marked their anniversary as the first timed they fucked, which was at one of those sex parties. He tells his kids that security staff in retail clothing stores only greet you so you know they're watching you. He passed as straight with a lot of people. He collected unemployment for months on several occasions. He was laid off from jobs. He ate fast food. He was asthmatic. He was diabetic. He had interstitial cystitis. He was spectrum. He worked day labor. He said he had chronic pain but he didn't look like it. He ate too much sugar. His youngest kid is a willful home schooled and unschooled kid who talks kinda like a grownup sometimes. He owed $30 to the Oakland Public Library. It took him six years to finish undergrad. He was rude to me when I asked him how long it would take for me to get a cab in front of the hotel. His graduate student loans are in default. He didn't see a dentist regularly despite having insurance. He had unpaid parking tickets. He probably had done a lot of other things. They would have caught him for something eventually. He had it coming. The cops have to deal with this all the time. He should have known better. He deserved to die.

Jubilee Showcase
(for Aaron Muhammad)

They gasp
Gagging
Clutching pearls
Scooting uncomfortably back in their seats
Knuckles bashing into hip bones
Gasping [smucking]
Aghast at the revelation [you what?!?]
And stare in disbelief
This devil
This hot boy
But love my Good Son
Who made it abacost flair
The flare of my popped collar
The flair of jeans new and crispy
Beard freshly tapered
Wisp of sweet from the unscented
Dr. Bronner's soap
Unapproachable shoe game
[Spit-shined black Stacys are the choice today]
Sonorous
Resplendent in brown fits coordinated
With his eyeglass frames
As he frames the discussion

[Revum Deacon Doctor Sonorous]
A Father, divine
Divining ideas and concepts
So they be relatable to the saints
These saints in his presence as he presents
To these presents   they are gifts
These saints of
Midweek noontime Sunday dinner
Minus smell-good water, Doublemint,
Choward's Gum and wide hats
Are my part of my ground
So I stay open and receptive

Breakdowns to very last compound
Agency at The Agency
Singing for my supper
Signifyin
Fackin and
Crackin amongst this uncracking Black

No, babysista
It is not my thangmama
Just ain't
But I'm here to serve my peoples mama
I grew up on the west side of Chicago mama
With ya mamanem and babysistnem and cuz
[What yo mama say 'bout that boy?]

[Well you know them dashiki folk
the Garveyites and such
they luuuuuuuuuuuuuuhhtheload too quiet as it's kept]
So you you know you know ya mamanem
And so you know I'm kinda like
Uhhhhhhhh
Uhhhhhhhhh I lived across the street
Churchagoddincryst by default
Because I know all the songs all
Of Mahalia's all of Mattie Moss
And Milton Brunsons
And Tommies and William Everett Preston
WILL IT GO ROUND IN CIRCULLLULLS be unbroken
But I wrote a poem dat ain't got no morals
But that ain't cause I ain't got no center
Or compass or rudder
And they keep asking
How you know wrong from right, boy?

I guess
I have a sense
Somehow
But I do wonder about folks with books
Or particular sets of rules and admonitions
And imperatives
While I go for what I know
I know that that the gay babalao

Who helped me save my own life on video
Twenty-five years ago
As his already grayed locks swung at me
Through the tv tube
Following his Medusa Snap
Only sees his spiritual children when
They need a reading
Or the bones thrown
Never for groceries or a ride to the train
Or just a visit

Did
The Orishas call you?
Did
You see his disappointment on his face
Reflected in
Your fresh run dishwater?
Did the drum thunder clapback
Talk to you from the distance?
I can't hear him
But I will be shaking the maracas
At each of his altaros when
I come through the door, per protocol
And have a cup of Bustelo and a cookie
And remember to bring a Safeway card
And fruit because they sustain him

Back in undergrad
They hung out a lot in the K building
Always in the student union and cafeteria
No dorms on campus yet
So lots of Batman cartoons and bid whist
And microwave popcorn
And cheeseburgers in bags
After class
There are two long tables full of the saved
The born-again
The blessed and highly favored
Supping sodas and chips
Stretching fried fish and
American cheese sandwiches on wheat rolls
Bubble water and wine candy
Making a way
Through the just before payday
On the edge of Pell disbursement
Twin epidemics of Fundzalow Syndrome
And Pocketzemti's Disease
These twelve boys
Fresh from the circle jerk
In the basement of Cooley High
De-sy-poles DEE SY POLES
And this
One
Girl.

This
Unweeping Mary
This
Martha not moaning
She be sitting here
Everyday in this
Noontime repression ritual
This Seder of Sublimation
Because these choir boys with
Big Black Nuts   unfeasibly large testicles
Would never ever
Never think any of those
Nasty worldly impure
Unclean thoughts about
The sweat beading on her cleavage
Or the peach fuzz on her earlobe
That the sun glinted
Through the converted train yard building's stained glass
This Friday before Easter
Or her pussy pushing like a fist straining
Calling to me through the crotch
Of burgundy corduroy 501s
No, not a one of them.

That's for moi.
And.....I'm sorry.

I mean, I'm not sorry *yet*
She told me that I would be
That I should watch out
Because he was coming back
And he was angry
And jealous and righteous
And I would kneel before him
But she's stopped
Just short of saying
He's going to fuck
Your unbelieving heathenous face
With his holy glowing halo ringed
Monster Jesus cock
Right here in the student union
And I'm going to frig myself
Rub this one out through my pants
And crush both nipples
Through this bullet bra
And watch because
It would be decidedly un-Christian
To avert my gaze from this spectacle

Shirley Caesar would surely seize her
And that wouldn't be quite right because
Twinkie Clark is closer to her age
And *Mother Marion Barry*

Those *thighs*
But I'm getting off track here
That Devil is always at work ain't he now?
Where was I?
Ah, yes....

"Do you have a church home?"
"No."
"Why not?"
"Same reason I ain't got a mosque home
Or a synagogue home or an ashram home."

He's cracking up.
I think it's my stone face
And fuckyounigga smile
Our business is done
As he's clear that
I could seriously complicate
An impressionable ex-con's
Close walk with thee
And we don't need anymore
Long haired,free thinking dress wearing
Loose-bootied Potential New Boyfriends in the mix
So I'm left to my own devices
For the moment
In these little spaces between
And in larger ones off the clock

I will continue to collect toys
For my ceremonial bureau top
Lined with candles
Evergreen from behind auntie's house
Dirtfrom Mum-Maw's grave
Pictures of leather daddies, fuck buddies
And program supervisors gone too soon

We will name our baby after warbirds
And blue watermamas and trees
And cotton eyed coal miners
And singing about going up
The rough sides of mountains
And seeing Spanish angels
When Mom comes to town
Not giving a fuck
If it makes sense to Chris Hitchens
Or any other arrogant white boys
Who can't wrap their mind around
The Spirit of The Boogie
Or love like a holy ghost swinging
Or having to believe that we are magic
Is about having nothing
No one
Or two or three
Stand in the way of our ineffability.

I cannot love a lord
Because I am too busy loving you.

No Reservations

There is sidewalk barbecue for four dollars.
["Don't worry. Y'all gon eat, fam."]

Side order of elbow bump,
A for real hug and the brush of his beard
Cross my cheek that recalls
Both a kiss on the neck from Earnest Hite-
First man ever to call me boo,
And an initial capped Dutiful Parent,
[My sweet carefully reminds me
To remember his menschyness]
Who fed bites
Of a Hardee's double cheese with fries,
Simultaneously dabbing rivers
Of tears and snot,
Doing his absolute best to distract
An edge-of-thirteen son from
The brutal throb
Of a ring finger compound fractured
While bicycle racing down the holler
In a colored section of a colored section
Of West-by-God.

Memory commingles and weaves
Without consideration for my boundaries
Cemented in
Post-millennial counselor trainings
That instructed you in simultaneous
Loving and distancing of your brothers
["Slow down and wait until I git da greeze fo your legs."]

I want this to be easier somehow
More obvious -but he did say
That I will understand when I am bigger
Some time after the campus
Had been fully repurposed
Or leased to Le Cordon Bleu
And there is a condo with a Luluemon
Covering the central stockyard
Near Roosevelt Road
And fried bologna sammiches with ketchup
From White Palace Grill
That sustained them while throwing mail
In the third shift graveyard at the main

And that delicious hamburger steak
That was really just a ball of two patties,
Chopped scallions and salt and pepper,
And Impossibly fluffy-times-crisp

Potato pancakes At the lunch counter
Next to the Florsheim shoe outlet
Are displaced by way better coffee
And glorified roach coaches
In a wagon circle
Selling a smorgasbord of the latest
We-like-everything-about-you but-you-style
Cuisine

Magic Johnson

He keeps the wand zippered
Until just the right time
The precise moment
Surprise and attendant shock values being
Integral to the success of the performance
Rice boiled to a perfect al dente
Butter and syrup
Running over bubble-topped
Scorched earth trampolines
Up and over Belgian Congolese
Eggo-compartmentalizations
Salty-sweet oleosucrotic coagulation
In Tuesday morning TV spots
A crispy coating delicately locking in
Deep-fried, pepper-flecked anger
Subconsciously rubbed into
3,744 company store bought chickens
Desperately kneaded into virally-atrophied
Growth centers near closing
On knobby-kneed Mississippi girls
Sent home to die with they Mum-Maws

I guess I'm better off today
Hipster enough to be annoyed at the irony

Tag, you're it
Run Hopalong, Run
Aysie Mae is turning shades of pale
Weaving 'cross
Central Park Boulevard traffic
To scoop red rag bologna loaf
From a gutter corner stop
That was constructed
Especially for her brothers to stand on

It's the Miracle on Ogden
Meeting a $1.35-an-hour Spiegel Man
Ten years earlier and eight years too late
All in the same wormholing moment
Of a last poetic rip in time/space fabric
A patternmastering of checkerboard
And purple fleur-de-lis
Sewn into buba, gele and dashiki

Proto knee-ga-roe peering
Through tiny horned rims
Stomach rumbling around eleven-thirty
While contemplating the contradiction of
Allowing white Commonwealth Edison and People's Gas men
Into our Ancient Afrikan Storefront

Scraping clean the paper plate
Of curry powder, sugar, salt
And starches necessary
To survive the six months with no end
That predicated diabetic
And high-blood-pressured futures

Blood is now thinner than water
You've been soaking in it, girl
Rib bones float through a hot sauce cloud
To the ocean floor
A moment of truth above deck finds him
Frozen and indecisive
Contemplating the quiet ovah-ness
In the wet, blue dark
Waiting to consume the home team

Pulling up for a jumper, his feets fail
[The problematic missing big toe
That landed him on the disabled list last season]
Or is it the chain mail message,
An ankle-transmission
From the back of the line
Signaling a change in play

He can make
Five thousand and one things from a yam

Compress peanuts into phonograph needles
Make boogers talk
Last the sole to your last pair of shoes
While spitting up chunks of lung,
Defy gravity's laws
With the help of willows and oaks
Memorize the lay of
A town without pity for his folk
Teach the Shakers his Promethean recipes
For curling Sankofas and Gy-name
Out of hot iron
In any or all of those Lou Rawls-narrated
Anheuser-Busch-sponsored minutes
That got him through the 1980s
Transfused by
C. Drew's blood memorizations
And the knowledge
That he ain't supposed to die a natural death
And that despite
Overwhelming evidence to the contrary
It's going to be alright

On BART, making note to self.

"Self: do not get shot in the face
By SFPD today. It's pissing raining,
And it would be a little too
'Cornbread, Earl and Me'
[American International Pictures, 1975].
Wait 'til the summer, and it dries out a bit
So you can get a bit of that
'Do The Right Thing' style
Balmy evening action on....with pizza."

Three Different Streets

I.

You
Are a traitor
To your race, gender and culture
[That's what s/h/e typed,verbatim]
Among other sundry isms not long before
The camera started rolling
[Niggas be rolling, rolling, rolling...]
I received notice   more indictment[s]
That the abstract genitalia diagram
Of roofing nails on the wall of my loft
Would somehow corrupt the mind
Of my seed
In a manner that the "Street Woman"
On our living room wall
[An oil painted in 1968 in a downstate Illinois prison]
Managed not to become a Joliet Penitentiary
The 106 miles from Chicago
Distancing the corruption
Because it's OK and appropriate
For Negro Illustrators to paint

Urban Renewal Murals Encouraging Community Uplift
[Dad's parable: "If you stay in a whorehouse
Long enough you'll turn a trick, son."]
It's OK as long
As the tricks don't trick us with their Trickery
As long as we do not have to imagine
That they might be real people
Speak, exposit, cuss
Jump out of the varnished mahogany frames
And know where they goin' to
Pussy-popping at
Our pre-Kwanzaa dinner party,
Causing the Council of Elders
To spill box wine
On their leopard print dashikis
Mamaspeculation:
["I think he was probably painting a dude."]
As if saying so would make her
Less titillating,
Make nipples and lines of linae
And pubes look less tasty to me
Make them somehow less chock full of
Possibilities
Like the way Juneteenth let us know
It was gonna happen [lest we forget]

This be not the Sport and Play
Of the Asiatic Black Man

The middlesexing that made
Elijah Muhammad's dick jump
And got his asthma going
This is our way   the way
Our ironic and schizoid disgust
At our own spectacle[s]
Speaking when spoken to
My brain makes scenes that are not heard
But blood taps breakbeats
On the rhythm pad inside of my skull.

II.

The party is starting
[Taps forehead]
Up in here   up in here
Four 1982 dollars
Will buy an Italian beef sandwich
[bread dipped in au jus]
With a slice of American, ketchup on fries
And a large Suicide with extra ice
And will give a bit of time
For the host to stack
Penis-shaped soaps and vitamins
While the evening's entertainment
A Reggie Theus look-alike
With chest hair like spilled raisins

Disrobes in my bedroom
Mamasdirective:
["don't come back up 'til
The street lights iz on."]
I hope they tipped well, Reggie
But know they didn't,
Though they wanted to.
[they could not...that would be shameless...and they are the shame]
Reg learned me. I want to thank that brotha,
Thirty years on
For an age-appropriate germ
In my twelfth summer.

He showed up again later
Courtesy of stepdad's Betamax collection
Sneak-peeks into Sex Worlds
During parent's Saturday overtime
Featuring Special Guest Star
Mr. Johnny Keyes,
Looking like a
Black Nationalist/Pan-Africanist
Superhero fantasy
Sleeveless White lycra spandex bodysuit
Crotchless
With his pretty dick swangin' at my face
Afro flawless, barefoot,
Tiger tooth necklace nestled

On more chest raisins
[will be his um.....sidekick,
Yup, once my balls drop!]
And will fuck alllllll of his run-off pussy
Alllllllll of dem white girls
Just like Jackie Wilson's personal assistant
Told me he did, back in the day
Until that day
I will set the VCR and
Will not fast forward through my lessons.

II. ½

I am
Somebody
I'm a college graduated bohemian rapnigga
I got a baby mama
But we got in a fight
So now
I got a woman
Way over town
With a three-chip Sony
Oh yeah
And friends doing grainy art school movies
With a capital A
On Fisher-Price PXL 2000s

I'm a weekend dad
With lots of free time
And space and time and space
And illmatic head game
[Black men don't eat pussy yet, see]
That gets me whines
And crudite'
And a spot on an erotica tape loop,
Flickering, honey dripping from my nipples
Five minutes at a time
In a Barneys New York
Storefront window display.
No one ['specially baby mama] is the wiser

But I'm learning quickly
If not quite keeping pace
With the increasing computational speed
Of The School's post production equipment
An the post orgasmic shrinkage
That will eventually
Put the power of two in my hand.
It's all fine
Fun and games and art and beauty
And for The People
Until Vaseline-lensed scenes with
Gossamer-draped four poster beds
Give way to squirting and ass-fisting and

Brobdingnagian crotch shots
Your and your head is put out
And you can't with me anymore
And it becomes about "The Children"
As if an eight-year old boy
Now two thousand miles away
Give a shit about anything other than
How seldom he sees me
Or that his mom needs to give a shit About
Anything I'm doing
Other than whether it's something
That will get the back child support
Sent to her yesterday.

III.

["Is it hot? Check."]
["Do they write hot checks? Naw? Check."]
Then we all good
And they fitting to posterize this rapfaggot
I'm legendary
I'm nekkid
'Cept for my Starbucks apron
Piped dress socks
And black Stacy Adams wingtips
They call me El Grande Dark
'Cept I like to use my real name

So the kids
So the family
So the chirrens
So them that's in the life
Know there's no shame
But that there's a gang
Of middle-class privilege and insulation
That accompanies my
Alt-porn collar popping and academic swag

My li'l one
["Papa going to work tonight."]
Is spit on a skillet.
Whip-smart like her mama
[I got another baby mama]
Who be a fried squirrel 'n' beans eatin' Missouri mischling
With a raft of hiding from DCFS
Trepidation-cum-terror
Inherited from her own mama.
Unlike my
Talented Tenthian proto-negro self,
And my 1964-bits of civil right
Mixed blood dyke trashgirl attorneys know
That the law is what is done
So she tell me to bring home stories
Teach them chirren well
Swang that dick

Wire that grocery and rent money
Watch your Black ass, baby
Cuz we love your black ass
Be careful on tour with that gang of hoes
Especially when riding through Scottsboro
And hug them
Because I love them hoes, too
And love comes quick.
Coins come in a hurry.
We git it done
No waiting on student union admin
To cut us loot

My boy is now old enough
To guess what his dad's steez is
But we still have the formal conversation
As I'm hyper-conscious
Of leaving things unsaid
["Yeah Dad, I kinda guessed from the spines of the dvds on the
shelf."]
I'm getting to that age now
Summer short suits, piped dress socks
Mint and toothpicks in shirt pocket
Unlit Kool Menthol
Rapidly bobbing on the bottom lip
'Cause I'm too busy shit-talking to light it
Driving it home

Leaning back
Burgundy sedan be immaculate
Egyptian Musk air freshener
From the record store
Hanging from the rear-view mirror
Leather seats polished and
Important Papers tucked
In the passenger side sun visor

["You know what this is, boy?"]
["Yeah, dad...issa check."]
["It ain't jussa check, boy."]
Teenage eyes roll like Vegas slots.
["What is it, then?"]
["It's a car note."] ["It's from a job."] ["It's work."]
["It's always work."] ["It's good."] ["It's real..."]
["And fuck *anybody* that ever tries to tell you different."]

14th, across

On Broadway
The young contextual wasp
On the way home
To the sketchy but affordable sublet
Hears the grandmama moan
In the bus shelter
It puts all on alert
That her soul's train is scrambling
In this yard at dusk
And before I know it
A future trophy wife from Vassar
Has gotten thee behind my back
Hoping real hard that
I will recognize my duty to her pulchritude
That I will rise up
To protect her inner Mae West
Cross this state line just two steps away
Coated in my Unforgivable
That Hetfield sang of in ninety-two

Bike bag and Target sack filled
With leftover pizza and home test kits
Nothing of use for an old blacklady

In her one for the bus-fared,
One for the jukebox
Killer Joe duck-walking, she
Through the early evening traffic gaps
Railing and fist shaking
Spitting tongues at The One 'bout how
You don't know nothing
You don't know nothing bout
'Bout these fourteen T cells
And lack-a-lack and more

She rides
And rides
Cackling intermittently
Satisfied
To the East, my brothers
Where tomorrow's scheduled
Follow-up appointment
Is the least of the concerns
Way way down in that Lonesome Valley
Near the bottoms of the queue

Not Yet Uhuru
(for the children of Thomas Equiano)

equiano acho   equiano acho
where am i
where is equiano
he's out
working on it don't you see him
see the kids riding my pony
crop in hand   bit in mouth
smarty art smarting at kicked haunches
while spurs jingle jangle jigaboo time
so good at it
they made james evans' seniority disappear
for uppity finger waves
about making jj look stupid
we continued to watch the asphalt grow
after florida dropped the punch bowl
asphalt growing blacker and worn to gray and blacked again
with that new hot pressed smell, like my tar baby's armpits

gotta have that fonk
gotta have gotta have
gotta have gotta haaaave
power

salt licked from wax bootblacked
spit and sprayed and pop-snapped
and bird smeared with kiwi
swabbed with the shinola
that i know from shite even when
i don't know where i am, equiano
[where are you]
we is
waiting next door he is
the man sitting next to the man
sitting next to the man
sitting next to the man
sitting next to the motherfucking man
sitting next to man-o-war and man-at-arms
and men who master this universe
through the power of skull-fucking
[hammer, hammer, i am]
they put me in the mix
when it's time to party with the lights out
we get it started
by revolving around
the one white boy holding the bulb

it's dark in this bathroom here equiano
but i can still see
cause my jacked johnson
is shiny and sweaty

reflective
and yo, we are paperweight champs
pillars of coal
he be two hundred fifty pounds of clay
unforgivably black but still necessary
this bridge called my dick
call all of mine   like you call me
george   emmitt   boy
schwerner   chaney   goodman
bayard   strayhorn   marlon
jimmy   ernest everett   gary fisher
call me detroit red the junkiemaker
punking hypes kneeling for swizza
before i hajj to your mecca

slow down, bro no hurry, take it easy
[how long? not long.]
the bart will get us from africa to fairyland
in no time flat
to here nor there is what i is
a nice idea
yet complicated in execution
though simple to execute
cain't step outta skin or history
emancipated into conscriptions
this new south of my own choice
no chay-yay-yains to keep us together

we are each others backdrop
each others suspension of disbelief
[the world is very different now]
i's free   eyes free
free at last
to niggerplay with race bannon and dr. quest
inhibition and prohibition
melting away in clouds
of poppers and shitstank
that morph into cartoon question marks
over my head
such as
since they took the doors off
the stalls in the bath,
why do i still need three i.d.s
to get in the club?
because it's midnight, son
at the midnight sun
ask them at the catacombs
you were there,whether you know it or not
seen you sprinkled in a few snapshots
pepper flecking a bowl of hot grits
here and again
[though they would have preferred more refined sugar]
imagining many of you squeezing twixt
ya mamamems's blond jesus jesus jesus hallelujahgobbles
and falcon man action ken's

alternating fetishization and loathing
but essex taught me to think when i fuck
and i'd be better off if
i didn't pretend that i didn't want it
when i know i want it
know i *need it*, equiano

so the remaining unburnt brain cells
will pitch-shift
from top to bottom to top to bottom
to my master slash daddy
in eighty three north cali
to my master slash daddy
five generations ago
in tillatoba, mississippi
see, i got pictures of both

you feel good good good
and pat yourself on the back
of your $875 vest
'cause there's consent here
[and the world is very different now]
no need to imagine or speculate as to whether or not
sally hemings' pussy was popping
if she was getting off in her scenes
[you've convinced yourself that was so]

or what safeword[s] tom sawyer and jim might have agreed upon
just swapping out
that coffee can of bacon drippings
for fresh crisco is enough

allow me to slather
this creaminess up my arm
imbuing myself with meaning   relevance
preparing to pretend to be able
to punish it through punishing you
though given the visual one is more likely
to imagine it as
kunta kinte amputated to the elbow
ass eating and sucking his otherness

[dude, i heard the glove he's wearing is the same one that black track guy
raising his fist wore at the medal ceremony in the
sixty-eight olympics in mexico city
that's soooooooooooooooooo hot]

affirmative action engendered quota
of hot space and time
and time and space left
for a last poet to metaphorize your insides
understanding that
no matter what we say to each other
the fact that we are both here

makes you not one of them
and that will be apparent
when the lights come up
when we are forced into the street
and the upstanding
wine cheese and crudite segments
of what we thought was our community
[or your community at least]
shows us and every brother ain't a brother
[though i already knew that]

so what you thought was your community
will blame us   me and you
will blame both the darkness and the light
will blame everything in between
will blame the buttons on your cap
will blame your motorcycle shades
will blame the rag in your pocket
will blame
the dried piss streaks on your chaps
will blame sylvester and giorgio moroder and kraftwerk and fantasy
records
and every arrogant italian disco producer who ever lived
for the pants and boots bass lines
that kept the time

they will blame us both

for the tongue cancer and cmv
will blame us for the crushed grape
on my cousin's temple
will blame us for your sister's neuropathy
will carry on and on
in trite and all-too-ironic
public humiliation scenes
begging and pennant
and yes sir may i have another
and uncle tomming to straight people
yes sir may i have another
for the nasty nasty behavior
of their freaky dinge-loving
and/or snow queening cousins
[both of whom they like to fuck in secret]
goosey goosey   guinea guinea
kinfolk pussy   good as any
apologizing for the least of us
the unsavory shameless bohemian elements of our kind
the secret meetings around the slings
and st. andrew's cross
with the selfish selfish addicts
and the lone representative from haiti
who have unleashed this plague
upon your progeny
that would certainly have been held at bay
had they not used so many dirty words

and done it so violently and loudly
and had done it all in their bedrooms
and had gone away quietly
and in all their complications
and contradictions
and sickness inside of sickness
and made it simple for you
and had allowed you
to continue to blame them

but that happens sometimes you know
when people don't pay
close enough attention
because it's all always pretend
just playing
an edgy artistic expression
when mapplethorpe kept
chopping your head
outta the frame, equiano
or maybe he was just remembering
paying attention
to something he was s'posed to
compelled to
but even if he was just benighted as fuck
it sho as hell didn't take
a coffee table book fulla gelatin plates
to get the point across

tell me where you ended up
in this middle after the middle
just passing through once
was enough to know i'm in this same place
that i've been for so long stuck
between a rock and my hard on
man on film jerking off
cross the world
from north lawndale to finland
and wondering how long we can deal
with being the rain on their parades
and hoping neither of them see me
because i know that
they can't actually stand to see
me

Re/membering Mamuwalde

[Look the other way when he come by you]
[Look the other way when he come by you]
[Look the other way when he come by you]
[Don't let him follow through]
      [from "There He Is Again"
by The Hues Corporation,1972]

It was the best of times
And it was the best of times
Chris Lee had a hammer
Brothers and sisters
Working out   Glad to be
Working
Northwestern Football Fred Right Said
Cigar dangling
Dangling

"I am not exploited in my exploits"
[Spearchucking]
"I am working" [jonesing]
Mean[s] Johnny Barrows getting paid without his chemistry degree
But never without them three degrees of

Chemistry
My daddy sings
The old way
Not of sixteen tons but of seeing Joe Hill
And of blood signing names
And how he knew 'cause Jesus told him
He had been there/owed him a quarter
Old as dirt
                    Mythrian
                    Everlasting
Song staying the same
Through the leave some/take some
Though that's not how men are inclined
To do, you know
So William works
Though he's only a bill
Waiting to be made law
Wanting to be real
Not cartoon
More than the one drop
Battyman dandy
Chasing silhouetted white go-go booty
Cross gene [page] code bits posterized
But failing to make it into the can
William Marshalling the dignity
Flyboy in the buttermilk
His own page in the Star Trek Wiki

Top gun in the company
Of ensembled negroes
Master thespian never ever merely
Acting
Ceremonial dark old man
Reading ingredients on peanut butter jars
Into Shakespeare
Dignifying everything with responses

The first response:
Antag to Arkoff's
Ugly American Internacionale
"I've never lost money on a picture"
[Never ever in the red]
[I keep things in the black]
[Keep bringing in the green]
Green room exposition
Explanation:clarification
["I don't play standard grade sweetbacked Cuttaniggas"]
Must fill and fulfill
Resonate with
fulfillingness fulfillingness fulfillingness
Garvey in Denmark
Nat Turner in Blyden
Metaphor better for
Ultramagnetic emcee
Live on stage

Crisp and clean baritone
[No matter what you think]
[No matter what you see]
[No matter what you think you see]
This is [not] a pimp cape
I love [these] hoes
Ebani Prince Billy

It's time to get free
Here for the
People the people
The people people the people
Africans at home and a broad
One God, One Aim, One Destiny
Boatloads of good intent
Roads paved with dead nigga skullbones
[Watch your step] else plans go awry

This cursed foil foiled again
A movement derailed
Love-starved love
Starved   hungry   delirium
Long time gone   long time coming
It's taking me so long to come
Two trains running
Transylvania to Lalaland
No irony in the awakening facilitated

By our metamiscegenating artfaggots
Just out of my mind   and into the night
Down Pico   Up Crenshaw
Nightclubbing with Grace
Your Jamaican Guy
Pulling up to your bumper
Closer to my Luva
                    Aching
Driving in between
Cows for your reincarnated milk
Milky
I'm back
["Vonetta is sparkling as the doe-eyed Tina," the tool at Variety
quips]

Mamuwaulde wants you
The right way
And wants you to want him too
But the jig is up
And there is no room at the inn for this
Big big big love
This timeless can't see to can't see
Or for the Tukansi
Or for the Motisa
Among these New Negroes
[Though there will be an Image Award]
They have found their heaven

And slammed the door behind
Chased you back to the big house
No thank yous
No justice
No peace
But dignity

[We will be taking our leave]
Gotta getaway
Gotta do it now
Gotta walk into the sun.
Hot.   Hot.
Made my choice.
Trading in my life.
Broken through to the otherside
But A.I.P. is in the blackety
So we have to go back
Drac
And do it again   to the beginning
Coffy is the color of her skin
Do as mama do   say as mama say
She ain't right or real he say
The blood didn't sign her name he say
I'm the number one sun, he say
[But you take life boy/you ain't one of us]
[You like all the biters]
[All the lines, all the rhymes]

[Leaving the rest]
[This is about family]
[About home/about spirit]
[You throw bones like they are cheap dice]
[Spill cherry Kool-Aid]
[Splashing the ground in a libation of lies]
[Cuz you wanna run thangs]
[Snatch me out my sleep for your]
[Don Cornelius scramble board bullshit]
Afroshit
Ultrashit
And
Ultrashit Cosmetic
Re-wrapped me in skin
          Out my peace
Away from bliss   Away from she
Where all had burned away
And I   And I
And you.   I *neeeeed* you.
Remind me of that haunted house
I once was in
And he can't leave unless she helps him
Find his way
Straightman
[In these proceedings, at least]
Can't play it cool no more
Dark

I don't wanna wait for this life to be over
I must suffer fools
Lay in wait   Lie in state
I suffer for you
No tale to tell
Body held like rag doll
Spiral dancing under the chandelier shots
Again
Anew
[Look the other way when he come by you]
[Look the other way when he come by you]
[Look the other way when he come by you]
[Don't let him follow through]

Seeing

(Smokey Robinson does *Pagliacci*)

Won't act like
I always know

What to do with myself
Three in the morning Chinese food after
Tangling in Black Sheets
Wrapping was easy
I hate Bill for withering
Hate him for moaning/mourning
Morning so right
In everyday darkness
I hate   cold tight fear in my chest
Not like it used to be
Back in the day but still real
Hating how it makes me feel
Stupid.
Mean.
I know what you mean
Hating that I need reassurances
Wanting arms and
Spooning and
Whispers squeezing away terror
Deer in headlight

Hearing a foghorn on the psychic interstate
A boy frantically scooping
The frustrated last Rice Krispie
From the milk in a bowl
Of Ethereal Cereal

Am I at all interesting
A curiosity in admitting these moments
Of shitless fright?
I'm thinking too hard
It's time to lie in big bedded heat
Wait for the 10-minute rule
Counting other people's money
Paying the piper and pretending
I don't hop-skip bus to door to you
The loss of
Two hundred forty seven cool points
Being a bit much
Geek math notwithstanding

Wameru

Late for the study job
Where i contemplate
Bout the lil' thang-thangs
That doo rag bruh-bruh
Like him cross the aisle from me trades in
So despite his tea being clocked
He's right on time
Right next to sistah-girl
We gonna give our seats up to homeslice
His skinny youngin
Holding the right hand tightly
His youngest holding the left
Sitting in the wagon smiling while
Radio Flying to Sunnyvale

Shule Ya Watoto
(School is for Children)

February 5, 1972

The usable restroom to the rear left had a single commode, a soap streaked deco-gilded mirror, a gummed up wall-mounted powdered hand soap dispenser and a Mule Team hand cleanser-pitted face bowl that had seen at least four decades of cold-water splashes that crisped a menschy shopkeeper's cheeks and hid his homesickness and fading stamina from the afternoon customers. Today I imagine that there was also the soft, bleachy dogwood reminiscent aroma of young apprentice's daily rub-outs, a morphine rise here and there, secrets of little deaths shared between little women, a kid with pocket change counted and recounted for caramel candies, Now and Laters, Cherry Mashes or roller skate keys, plus innumerable lavender scented ho baths. The checkerboard tile floor is the only consistent motif of a recurring dream that I began having at age four. The dream does not abate until just before my twelfth birthday. It always begins with my attentions focused on a corner's ragged molding near the floor. A string of thick, inky, charcoal colored smoke slowly begins to curl up and outward from behind the toilet. I turn to leave and rattle the knob but someone has locked me in, or someone or something is blocking the door from the other side. The smoke, which has no smell or taste, continues to billow, climbing upward and reaches me chest-high before I begin to silently panic and think to scream for help, but I always woke up right at that moment, in a light sweat and wondering if this was the beginning of

The Triumph of Black Nationhood that my classmates and I pledged our lives to every morning.

A Litany for Okonkwo

you and i
you and i
you and i
ceremonious dark men old and young
in the jungle the jungle
the Brothers the Brothers
lifted His Name (and that of others)
talked up the now 45 with .45s
for a score and a half
rock creek parking over boom bap
soul clap and trap
rolling with this flavor
despite the stomp to the nine zero's jump off
wilding out
with full page calls for Pentothal
despite

despite the warnings
despite the Lord's word of it
serving to remember
serving to remember
serving to remember
despite the warnings

of El[ie]El[ie]Cool W
to understand that
the bombing of tracks
did not and would not come from
the U.S. State Department
who knew the time
knew what was happening
yet sat it out back in nineteen thirty seven
despite the protestations
of the People

still my Brothers Brothers Brothers
long to be
Farrakhanian circumcisors of herstory
joy dividers despite our protestations
we been through this before
they keep saying
that the Maafa wasn't so bad
that the Maafa wasn't so bad
and besides

the flow of this stream
will once again be seen worldwide
is delivered in a black plane
spares us the indignity
of boat and/or train rides
includes meals and per diem
and pays by cashier's check

Dancing in
September

two faggots
stand stockstill in front of the screen
they be made a triptych by the third
who has again stumbled over his boundaries
this time out of the boudoir into the main
having been awakened piezoelectrically
by a thin-stringed muppet
[da plane, boss]
possessed of the idea that
this is a good eleven
that imperialist engendered proxy fundamentalism in brownface
somehow, someway = black revolution

lover
[and if it isn't love, why do I feel this way?]
she follows at polite distance
and with appropriate deference
per kyriarchic expectation-
though I don't quite have that word...yet
as things are falling apart in the East
and to the east
I feel blood beating in her fingers

heart hoping against hope for
some Holloway-style love
to go crashing as well
give this morning more meaning
straighten things out ['cause won't he fix it?]
provide more weight
and belie the happenstance of
running into my moms
at Nina Simone's last Chi-town gig
that led to our coinkydinky of desperate
cross-purposes in the summer previous

I would punch my Judys
who have managed to not piss the carpet Regan McNair-style
[three Cancer boys here, one thinks
bad look - already too much water in this room]
and they remain hypnotized
by the unfolding Shakatak
and I think better of hitting them
given the likelihood of busting knuckles
on their adamantine shoulders
or sinking so far into their solderly puddling
as to lose myself within
the commingle of our new terrors

luckily
there is the distraction

of the unannounced but expected
beta testing of hybrids
hauling ass down 69th street
we are two miles from the closed airport
one from the shuttered rapid transit station
and should we smirk and cluck tongues
while pouring milked oolong on the spectacle
we will be giving implicit and explicit assurances
that they are not afraid of us
for the moment

the nature of the threat
has brought us together
excluding and excepting
Mexican baristas with caterpillar eyebrows
high yallers with
Onondaga/Russian Jew grandparents
unlucky cabbies scraping by
in that Little Kabul
at the end of the Fremont line
and ice-veined neurosurgeons
eking it out
as shook-assed gameday hot dog vendors
because this is a tipping point
the prognosticators would have you believe
the solution for these screwflying Adamites
is to find someone

somebody
some new not-men to kill
after they've run out of girls and women.

L'authenticité

that spook Greenlee
spookily spoke
on the
existential limitations of
imitations of imitations
in nativist nativity scenes
availed of uh 'burg-heart hardened consciousness
that's double-time jointed
resulting in four funky dislocations
plus one more, if you will
[because I like the girls]

if you will, picture
a picture
six foot seven foot eight foot
[Bunch[e]]s
ralphing at the sight at the site
of buckets of right foots, left foots
opposing thumbs
maybe an ear
that one needs not to see
as it is the cost of this framing
of a center that holds, apparently
its edges gilded in Leopoldian cobalt blues

five black hand side-severed hands
phantom neuropathics banging synapse
squeezing baby-babays
from a time tested tube of Holbein
prepped for the palette's palate
onto newly stretched and primed linen
official portraiture
hanging on this pre-incursive line we passed
during the five-hundredth year of botany
sometime in the past two decades

let's try not to get too far ahead of ourselves
lest miss the mise en scène
of Kasa-vubu's laundry servants
razor creasing
the new president's Arzoni slacks
finishing them with light, gentle spritzings of lavender water
Sanforized waistband
eliminates gathering and pinch
pant leg hems folded and sewn just so
to gallop across a Montecassino loafer top
to the bottoms
and to the top
staring at the multitudes
in a full length mirror
trading John Foster Dulles lenses
pop-bottle thick

for nerd specs fancied mod Malcolmite
staring down at
a million upon a million upon a million
in a recursion of abacosts
multitudes dreaming of
the possible and the might have been
the possible and the dreams
that might have been
the might of the dream
and all that we might have dreamed
folded gently into
an impossibly flaky
silky smooth leopard skin cravat
Duke creamed natural
topped by rakishly tilted
zebra print garrison cap
the ensemble completed with
proto-proto dashiki inspired
neo-colonial topcoat
accented by cufflinks, lapel pin
and cane handle
whittled into appropriate shapes
from hydrochloric acid-polished Lumumba-bone.

A Little Bit of (Soap)

i can hear your asshole
singing to get filled up with supper
a raspy channeling of David Ruffin
the tenor of the Secrets bookstore booths
on Telegraph Avenue
with the dirty floors
the employee restroom
with the door removed

no privacy here
so we practice 'round the outside
hallways vestibules
and pissy hood foyers with
acoustic tiles bouncing vocal fry
singing an octave out of range
octave out of range to get that sound
whistle registering on tiptoes
because it's so good
temptation[s] cheering you on in
a pitching, chirpy doo-wop circle

in the good old days of the movie palace
when we sat in the peanut gallery
throwing half masticated nut chews
at the back of
miss ann's and mister charlie's children's heads on the main floor

respectable white gentlemen would
excuse themselves
just before the second reel
to head to the lower level for a shoeshine
or Jujubes or popcorn
take a place along the row of art deco gilded boxes
["men" in stainless steel caps lest there be any confusion]
grunt and adjust the fedora or
toe-tap or jingle jangle jingle a belt buckle
to signal for assistance
and begin the release of the tensions
of big business and modern industry

he wink-winks and flips a quarter
to my great grandfather
who is sitting on a stool
next to the trick towels
washes the memory and
sweet dogwood smell away
with Boraxo powder
grabs a handful of peppermints

and heads back to sit with his none-the-wiser
he doesn't want to confuse things
and my great grandpa
has his own things to do

by the time i came along
the grindhouse marquees
up the block from the bus station
were talking back in broken neon code
sixes replacing fractured nines
threes replacing e's
it runs together and i'm imagining
Blacula making out with Jim Kelly
while standing over Preach who is trying to scream Cochise back to life
under an "L" train
brakes screeching and dragging his soul away from Cabrini

and now there's liquid soap
but never quite enough
and never ever any towels
and instead of peppermints
there's eight balls
but they're not free
but we still doo-wop
and there's more time because
there's three kung fu movies
and no one will make you leave this place until the last reel because

the mama manager knows we need
someplace to sing
to be quiet to be private
and to touch each other and to get clean

a photo of these places
this glommed flickering corner
is speaking color uncorrected
in my fifth grade social studies book
near a side paragraph
about big city downtown
and the scary dangerous things in toilets
that your boy Leroi
both did and didn't imagine
Greenwich Village had plenty of all

there he was standing
there in the entrance ramp
took me when it was taken
that morning we left for St. Louis
and i tighten my eyes and see his
shorts so tight
and she see him too
i did and she knew i did
because she squeezes my hand and
his cut-offs are
gripping legs freshly greezed

and cascading sockless delicately ho bathed
    [the sink in Wabash or in the stall at Pacific Garden Mission?]

did he save any sins while he was there?
in those crisp white boat shoes
dancer-cut sweat top
thumbs hooked in belt loops
a Hershey-brown sentry with two kisses
peeking from sleeve-side
as his arms akimbo suggesting
to my greenness
that this giant mister is
clean
greeting guiding leading
    slipping into my future

there's a dick-print tight interspersed with
shhhhhgghhhhshhh
in the instant
you're gonna love it in an instant
nibbling the lunch Oreos surreptitiously
during my reading class
i'm all of seven but I give level six reads

and my face must have clearly
shown that i grabbed the possibility
the endless what could be

because next came
the terse whispered thatboyisaprostituuute
which i immediately understood as
this is something i should think is bad
but you don't push back with
but he so prettyshhhhhhhhhhhhhhhhhhhhh
when you elevenshhhhhhhhhhhhhh
in Car Wash she didn't have any lines but
she cleaned up in the sink and it was ok
    she lived 'til the end of the movie

we are standing
boys and girls single file at opposite ends
of the converted basement lunch area maze of cinderblock
grates and corrugated metal floors
and creosote paper coated pipes
and that weird boy Craig
Williams or Frazier
    i can't remember

he somehow managed to always
every fucking day
get to the very front of the line
and run without slipping
and slamming into the concrete wall
speed racing to stand on the floor drain

straddling the slant between each row of eight urinals
    pointing at each

that's a boy that's a girl
boy girl boy girl boy girl boy girl boy girl
uhnnnnn you with a boy
uhnnnnn you with a boy
gleefully play pissing
up a ceramic metapussy
uhnnnnnmmmm with a boy
sssssssdsshhhhhhhhghhhhghhhhhhhhhh
with head turned over shoulder
gaptooth grinning while sussing out
which of us was in the ass he'd designated as *oooooooooh*
but not as off-limits

powdered soap still struggles
to escape from a long caked dispenser bulb
that worked for white people
and tri folded waxed paper
gets balled in handfuls
that don't dry anything
in the doorless stall
with the sharpened serrations
on the overhanging bar
    to keep the chimps from swinging

at the foot bar-triggered sink
i wash and wash and wash
singing Rick James something or other
that i quietly bleed
into the Monty Python theme music

fingers still smelling lightly
of that funk the older boys on bikes
with banana seats
   leave on the wind

by the time it's a real thing for me
i'm way too saditty to kneel
too hip hop to fuck up my new pants
and too oblivious in moments to peep toe taps and cues except for
that one
that time we were at
North Avenue Novelties
Ron was way prettier than me
but he didn't know any better either
so he followed me into the stall
and got freaked out when
the dude started with his finger in
the screwdriver-hacked gloryhole
   with the dried shit-dribbles

i couldn't let on that he was

getting in the way of what i was feeling
but so is a May wedding and
that eight inches of snow outside

my boy Ra like the loo at
the downtown Oakland Sears
the Palace Hotel in San Francisco
and toilets at private colleges
while we were on tour
because he says they're way more
repressed and urgent and
i presume will fuck ones face
harder going *shhhhhhhhghhhhh*
and keep on singing
keep on singing
i remember my first drink at The Eagle
seeing a trough pissoir the first time
and thinking
wow this is like a triage or staging area
  before the stall

Craig
Frazier or Williams
i still don't remember which

  would have *loved* this

Twelve Forty
Three A.M. (Home)

axillaries wet
cold force vodka tonics
through pores
following a supper sing
key tapping
creeps me closer
than the eight hours
away from your arms
peace found after
flea flicking bits of small intestinal anx/iety
attaching to villi
digesting a once swallowed
constant old burn
clarity be a motherfuck
in that good kind of way
and taste of the inside
of the bottom lipid
you bite in moments
when the ache frightens you
and warms your chest
like the milk tea you sip
on one of these 1000 mornings past august
i want next to you

Dancing

she say
comeback before Wodens
if you like
or have the minutes
really wanting to scream
i love you
his response is layered
with secret agent comportment
to hide the sweating aches
as the Man of Tomorrow
watches from the easy chair
smiles at the two children afraid of flame
both shouting a chorus of "who me" while
steadily
caplonking lighter fluid 'pon the embers

How To Eat To(mato)

The sister said that it happened
During their annual Your Farmland Retreat
On the Nation's spread
Near Sandersville, Georgia
That the Messenger
[Elijah, the one prophesied to come]
Bought before his departure
That journey he took
Back in February of 1975
To that big wheel turnin' in the sky

Every Muslim Girl Trainee
The entire membership of
The General Civilization Class
Was all in pain, she said
Agony, agony in their bodies
Their hurt locked harmoniously
Children of the sun
Sweltering, suffering in their heat

Until that delicious moment
When Brother Minister

Walked onto the veranda
Flanked by two fresh-faced Fruit
And with smooth, effortless ceremony
Raised his left hand,which he'd cupped
Into a beauty queen's
Motorcade Waving Position

With his right
He reached into his opposite jacket pocket
And pulled out
A shining Heirloom variety
Held it forward
For his audience's perusal and approval
Then raised the plump fruit to his mouth
And plunged his perfect white teeth
Into the redness

Miraculously
All aching dissipated
Their release coming
Only a moment after
Their Saviour had arrived

reading guide

Theme: DIASPORA

MAA'FA

Despite having grown up in early-to-mid 1970s Africentrist education, I didn't encounter a drilled-down specificity of the contexts of the Transatlantic Slave Trade that gave a hint of its' indescribable and incomprehensible horror and awfulness until encountering media made in the 1990s (the films Beloved and Amistad come to mind) I watched the mini-series version of Alex Haley's Roots as a six year old in late 1976 (and seemingly endless reruns in the four years after) but it took me until rewatching of one in my late 40s to watch again and contemplate the individual experiences that were represented (Madge Sinclair's Binta, describing 50 years on the plantation and never having been past the tree line 1,000 feet away, comes to mind).

Attempts to dive into my notions of this are made difficult by my own moments of brain freeze at the incomprehensible day-to-day horror and my wanting to acknowledge with respect and give witness.

I have photographs of my maternal great-great grandfather who was born into slavery in 1857 and want to make that heard beyond personal and overcultural cliche. It's a particular kind of work to let go of the inclination to hand wring over it and just say the words and let them fall as they might.

Prompt:

- What is the oldest generational narrative that you have access to?
- Does it involve photographs or writings or sound recordings?
- If they are all oral, how might have they changed or transmuted upon passing from generation to generation, if they have?

Representative Poems:

- "Magic Johnson" (p. 27)
- "Three Different Streets" (p. 32)
- "Re/membering Mamuwaulde" (p. 54)

Prompt:

- Who has traditionally been responsible for the passing of oral and written narratives in your family?
- Has there been a formalized process or context for this transfer?
- If so, has it involved ceremony (formal or informal) or a discussion of how this was going to happen?

Representative Poems:

- "On BART "making note to self" (p. 31)
- "Shule Ya Watoto (School Is For Children)" (p. 65)
- "How To Eat To(mato)" (p. 87)

Theme: THE GREAT MIGRATION

There is a larger collectivized conversation about the 1910–1970 experience of Black migration from the southern United States to northern cities and the effects and experiences of that across the period mentioned in Isabel Wilkerson's historical study *The Warmth of Other Suns*. I found myself so viscerally struck by the intro and first chapter that I had to stop and pick a time to return as I felt myself inside the little boy who the moments on the train at night were being told from the perspective of.

The constancy of my personal narrative of this has been largely defined by being a first generation Northerner (my father grew up in a colored-only mining camp in West Virginia before permanent migration to Chicago after college graduation in 1960; my mother moved from southern Mississippi, for polio healthcare, in 1943, to Missouri, then Indiana, followed by East St. Louis, Illinois, before arriving in Chicago in 1949. The near west side of Chicago contained the larger number of new migrants; at my birth my mother had been a Chicago resident for 21 years, my father for 10.

Prompt:

- How do the chronological contexts of parents and the immediate geographical circumstance(s) of birth affect our notions about movement and migrations and connections to them?

Representative Poems:

- "Not Yet Uhuru (For the children of Thomas Equiano)" (p. 44)
- "Dancing In September" (p. 69)

Prompt:
- How do the above mentioned contexts affect our notional and relationships to "the land" and "the hood" (south side vs. West Side, tenement living vs. housing projects and single family homes?

Representative Poems:
- "14ᵗʰ, across" (p. 42)
- "Le Authenticité" (p. 73)

Theme: QUEER DIASPORICS

I left Chicago in December 1998 by train, on a trip designed with intent to arrive in the San Francisco Bay Area on January 1, 1999.

Though I'd had discussions with my then-partner about what I wanted to do once establishing roots (I'd discussed the possibility of writing and illustrating for bisexual magazine Anything That Moves as a starting point) we never had any substantive conversations about the general historical overlaps of Black and queer migrations to Northern California, let alone the specifics of Black LGBTQIA contexts of movement and how that may have informed our decisions and notions in ways we were yet to understand.

For myself, there was certainly an unwillingness to look head on at some things that were being navigated in large part due to uninterrogated dynamics of gender, class, and a 20-year age difference that informed each of our relationships to our natal communities. They left a marriage in a small town a state over, a mom to now grown children, and not formally "out" as queer; me, having recently divorced, parent to a kindergarten-aged child and having a recent deep estrangement from my parents.

That said, it was that much easier to stay focused on the magical and fantastical notions of migration as opposed to the more difficult "nuts and bolts" day-to-day jobs, housing life-space differences that were thrown into sharp relief by the move.

Prompt:
- What does it mean to reform/reframe/rebuild with the presumed ease of doing so in a space where no one knows you or your name/names?

Representative Poems:
- "An Ode to No Hearts (Pulse)"(p. 1)
- "No Reservations" (p. 24)
- "Dancing in September" (p. 69)

Prompt:
- What are the complications/implications of said movement on the edge of a functional consumer internet that at that point included no record of your previous identities as you'd been navigating life under your legal name as opposed to your given names that you know yourself by?

Representative Poems:
- "Dark Brother" (p. 5)
- "Not Yet Uhuru" (p. 44)
- "Shule Ya Watoto" (p. 65)

Theme: MEMORY

The process of reading through poems as a single body has led me to larger conversations with myself around how trauma informs memory. I began to think in specifics around what one qualifies as trauma based upon how it affects how one is able to tell, or is compelled to tell a story.

Prompt:
- How has your memory of shared familial events differed from that of your siblings? Cousins? Parents?
- What do you feel are the factors and variables that may have affected that? Age? Geography? Classed relationships across time?

Representative Poems:
- "Re/Membering Mamuwalde" (p. 54)
- "Shule Ya Watoto" (p. 65)
- "Dancing in September"(p. 69)

Prompt:
- What have been the recurrent themes that tie these memories together?
- What is the basis on which we decide what is kept as a collective memory, and how is that articulated?

Representative Poems:
- "Three Different Streets" (p. 32)
- "L' authenticité" (p. 73)
- "A Little Bit of (soap)"(p. 76)

Theme: IDENTITY

Both my parents have navigated contexts of chronic illness and disability since childhood but neither have ever formally identified as such. I have been chronically ill on some axis or other since childhood, but the notion of myself as such was elided by narratives of Afrocentricity/ Black Nationalism that did not allow for frailty or sickness in the building of Black Nationhood. "Sickness" was often used as a stand-in term for "whiteness," "homosexuality," or any behavioral modality that was "other" than appropriately "Black" but ironically steeped in white Supremacist narratives of verity connected to the appropriately masculine "(cis)Black."

Prompt:

- What notions or ideas connected to specific cultural frames or identifications have shaped where you come from?
- How have purity mythologies contributed to your notion(s) of self, and whether or not that self was worthy or "good"?

Representative Poems:

- "An Ode To No Hearts" (p. 1)
- "An Eminem's Front" (p. 4)
- "Julyteenth" (p. 12)
- "Wameru" (p. 64)

acknowledgments

Son of Byford would not have been born without the support, joy, anger, "facking and cracking," shade, love, intellect, blood, sweat, piss, vinegar, perseverance, and more of so many people. Some are listed here but there are so many who are not named because I don't know their names—they have given to me nonetheless.

Special thanks to Paul Corman-Roberts for encouraging me to submit my manuscript to Nomadic Press, and to J. K. Fowler for believing and giving it a home. Impossibly deep and effusive thanks to the BRILLIANT Noelia Cerna for her literal line-by-line guidance, attention, skill, thoughtfulness, and thoroughness as an editor. It is an amazing and rare privilege to have attentions given to one's work such as I have received from you, Noelia - thank you for supporting me and in seeing my jive and snatching my own edges. Big thanks to Laura Salazar for her initial and ongoing logistical support of the project, and to Michaela Mullin for her sharper-than-sharp readings near the end of the process.

To Oray Booker Washington (1888–1973), for rubbing the life back into my mama's polio-stricken body in 1943 Mississippi goddamn, and carrying her across state lines when they said, "take that li'l nigger home and let her die there."

To Mama (Kemba Johnson-Webb) and my dad (Joe Louis Johnson, Sr., aka Mzee Kambon Adilifu) for the gift of lettered and unlettered wisdom, the spoken and written word, shelves of books, piles of Ebony, Jet, Sepia, and Negro Digest magazines, Golden Legacy comics, records and tapes, the west side of Chicago, and windows to the world outside. Lazy hagiographies often deny the humanity of those subjected to them by deburring their edges and complexities. Thank you from the depth for your best even in the moments we have departed and disagreed- you are loved and appreciated.

To he who was stepdad in name only, Manuel Webb (1931–2018), and my paternal grandfather, Henry James Johnson, Sr. (1892–1976). You were and are my Working Class Heroes.

To the mamas of Shule Ya Watoto (1972–1990) for your rafts of unpaid emotional and physical labor on behalf of your babies. Black things today and Black things tomorrow...yes I will, one more time.

To the teachers and students of William H. Byford Elementary School (1977–1981) who held each other and held together in that time of great local and global transition.

To the students of House "D," of Frederick A. Douglass Middle School class of 1983, for your grit, and allowing me to represent you.

To the Black and Brown students from Lane Technical High School class of 1987. Thanks to the Black teacher cohort who held and helped a psychologically and emotionally fragile teenage boy believe he was good enough. I give particular thanks to the tenderness and fierceness of Mrs. Regeta Slaughter, Mr. Claude Grace, Mrs. Audrey Scott-Kelley, and Mr. Joseph Montgomery. I wouldn't have gotten through without their support through constancies of institutional racism, microaggression, and antagonism.

To Professor Robert Weitz and the Chicago State University (CSU) Art Department,

CSU head baseball coach Kevin L. McCray, to my advisors Walter Perkins and Derrick Baker and the staff, colleagues, and the CSU Tempo newspaper, where I cut my expository writing teeth from 1989-1993.

To my comrades and collaborators in the art of community: Deep Dickollective (D/DC), Linda Howard Valentine and the *Anything That Moves Magazine* staff, Patty Berne and Sins Invalid, Mangos With Chili, Matt Wobensmith (Outpunk Records), Judge Muscat and Rainbow Flava Soundsystem, Mama Rae Jones, Alex Hinton (Planet Janice Films/Pick Up The Mic), Kriss deJong and Eliot K Daughtry of Killer Banshee Studios, Scenes Unseen, PeaceOUT World Homohop Festival, Don Sappington/Raw Material, The Living Earth Show/COMMANDO, Annie Oakley and performers of The Sex Workers Art Show, Cris Sardina and Desiree Alliance, and the staff at St. James Infirmary.

To the poets who know it from the New College of California (NCOC); department chair, Adam F. Cornford, who wouldn't stop bugging me for a whole year to apply to the MFA program, and the brilliant Tom Clark (RIP) for being a real one from my part of the west side.

To Abejide Ajayi-Wafula Johnson and
Morrigan Yemaya Laurel Johnson deManda,
the two most amazing things I will ever have taken part in creating. Thank you for letting me be your Dad and Papa. Dee-Dee-Doh to my Baconhead and Blih-Luh-Luh-Luh, little bird.

Thank you to Nalo Hopkinson, David Findlay, Lisa Carlotta, Lynnee Breedlove, Richard Loranger, Pete King, Charlie Jane Anders, Leah Lakshmi Piepzna-Samarasinha, Richard "Dick Deluxe" Egner, Dismas Rotta, Marvin K. White, and Louie Butler III, for showing up and showing out with your art, and for making a way for myself and so many other artists.

To and for my ancestors, named and unnamed, known and unknown; calling a few because that's how we do: Anita "Mama Kofi" Douglas, Osei Buford, Michele Abernathy, Patrick Rademacher, Tim Stüttgen, Frederick Antawn "Ricky" Penn, Jack Random, Ajene Muteman Buford, Donnell McDowell, Shannon Williams,Ntozake Shange, Bill Brent, Juba Mahiri, Bro. Hannibal Tirus Afrik, Marcie Bee Thomas, Rickey Williams, Fred "Freddy Frog" Thomas, Shafiq Muhammad, Lindsay "Unka Luke" Johnson, Mama Nzinga Medlock, Aaron Muhammad, Delia McIntyre, Atiim Willis, Mama Folami Stallings, Byron Mason, Kujichagulia Cage, Mama Arety Wicks, Howard Kenrick "Jace" Mills, Rodney Woods, Kaya Nati, Margaret Ann Allen, Laura Betty Johnson, Lawrence V. McAllister, Eugene Blackmon, Jr., Henrietta Sinclair, Paris Brewer, Bobby House, Thelma Grasty, Hewitt Grasty, Jr. Mama Tabasumu Gray, Linda Tero, Baba Kabaila Gray, Jimmy Williams, Marlon Riggs, Essex Hemphill, and Brian "BJ" Jones.

Finally, endless purple flowers, root beers, Black Sheets and August 10ths to Janine Marie deManda, for twenty years of undying love, passion, intellect, partnership, support, struggle, and encouragement. Thank you for helping me see and be my best self, and for continuing to be the amazing gift of a human you are to the world, querida mia.

Thanks to the following journal for giving an earlier version of this poem a home:

"Three Different Streets," in *Hustling Verse: An Anthology of Sex Worker's Poetry* (Arsenal Pulp Press)

Juba Kalamka

Juba Kalamka is most recognized for his work as co-founder and producer of homohop group, Deep Dickollective (D/DC), and for his development of the micro-label sugartruck recordings. His cultural work and writing centers on intersectional dialogues on race, identity, gender, disability, sexuality, and class in popular media. He served six years as a music columnist, book reviewer, and feature writer for *Colorlines* magazine. Kalamka lives in Oakland with his partner of 20 years, their daughter, a neurotic standard poodle, and an enthusiastically- territorial rescue dog. *Son of Byford* is his first book.

cover missive

On "Blue Figure"
by Wardell McNeal

Wardell McNeal is an Oakland-based visual artist, whose stylized figurative work depict unique universes of metaphysical meanderings. Their work encourages viewers to take pause and examine the complexities of existence, the nature of reality, and of being and becoming.

 @post_structure

Nomadic Press Emergency Fund

Nomadic Press Black Writers Fund

Right before Labor Day 2020 (and in response to the effects of COVID), Nomadic Press launched its Emergency Fund, a forever fund meant to support Nomadic Press-published writers who have no income, are unemployed, don't qualify for unemployment, have no healthcare, or are just generally in need of covering unexpected or impactful expenses.

Funds are first come, first serve, and are available as long as there is money in the account, and there is a dignity centered internal application that interested folks submit. Disbursements are made for any amount up to $300.

All donations made to this fund are kept in a separate account. The Nomadic Press Emergency Fund (NPEF) account and associated processes (like the application) are overseen by Nomadic Press authors and the group meets every month.

On Juneteenth (June 19) 2020, Nomadic Press launched the Nomadic Press Black Writers Fund (NPBWF), a forever fund that will be directly built into the fabric of our organization for as long as Nomadic Press exists and puts additional monies directly into the pockets of our Black writers at the end of each year.

Here is how it works:

$1 of each book sale goes into the fund.

At the end of each year, all Nomadic Press authors have the opportunity to voluntarily donate none, part, or all of their royalties to the fund.

Anyone from our larger communities can donate to the fund. This is where you come in!

At the end of the year, whatever monies are in the fund will be evenly distributed to all Black Nomadic Press authors that have been published by the date of disbursement (mid-to-late December).

The fund (and associated, separate bank account) has an oversight team comprised of four authors (Ayodele Nzinga, Daniel B. Summerhill, Dazié Grego-Sykes, and Odelia Younge) + Nomadic Press Executive Director J. K. Fowler.

Please consider supporting these funds. You can also more generally support Nomadic Press by donating to our general fund via nomadicpress.org/donate and by continuing to buy our books.

As always, thank you for your support!

Scan the QR code for more information and/or to donate.

You can also donate at nomadicpress.org/store.